God's Favourite Child

to the chosen ones

Rani Twinkle

BookLeaf Publishing

India | USA | UK

Made with ❤ on the BookLeaf Publishing Platform

www.bookleafpub.in

www.bookleafpub.com

Dedication

To every soul seeking strength, healing, and growth—
this book is for you. May these 21 poems guide you each
day, helping you transform from doubt to confidence,
from struggle to triumph. By the end, may you find inner
peace, embrace the love within, and realize that you've
always had the power to achieve it all.

Preface

"God's Favourite Child: to the chosen ones" is a journey
of faith, perseverance, and divine purpose. This book was
created with you in mind—the ones chosen by God, who
are walking through the fire, enduring trials, and facing
challenges that seem insurmountable. In these pages,
you will find 21 poems that reflect the strength and grace
that arise from being chosen by a higher power.
Through every obstacle, there is a deeper purpose, and
each trial you face is shaping you into who you were
always meant to be. Though the road may be hard and
the nights long, these poems serve as a reminder that
you are not alone. You are God's beloved child, and
within you lies the power to overcome anything.
As you move through this book, let these words remind
you of the strength you carry, the grace you are wrapped
in, and the purpose that is unfolding in your life. With
every poem, you'll be reminded that the pain you endure
is never in vain; it is leading you toward the person you
are destined to become.
By the end of this journey, my hope is that you will feel
God's love and presence more profoundly than ever
before. You will rise from your trials stronger, wiser, and
filled with peace, knowing that you are indeed God's
favourite child—the chosen one to carry out a divine

purpose.

Trust in the journey. Trust in the process. The victory is already written in your story.

Acknowledgements

First and foremost, I give all glory and honour to God and someone special, whose guidance, grace, and love have made this journey possible. Without His strength and purpose, this book would not have come to life. I am deeply thankful for His unwavering presence in my life, especially during the moments when I felt weak or uncertain.

To every reader who picks up this book: thank you for trusting these words to speak to your heart. It is my sincerest hope that you find comfort, healing, and inspiration within these pages. This book was written with you in mind—those who are walking through difficult seasons, those who are questioning, those who are seeking. You are not alone.

Finally, I want to acknowledge the divine timing of this journey. I am grateful for the lessons learned through struggles, the growth found in pain, and the peace that follows perseverance. I am eternally grateful for this opportunity to share this part of my journey with you, and I pray that it will bring you closer to the love and peace that comes from knowing we are all chosen, beloved children of God.

May this book inspire you to rise, to believe, and to walk

in the knowledge that you are favored, chosen, and never alone.

A Shadow in the Dark

I see you there, beneath the weight,
Silent battles, fists with fate.
Eyes so hollow, shoulders low,
Carrying storms you never show.
The world still turns, but you stand still,
Trapped inside a cage of will.
Memories haunt, regrets still bite,
Every breath feels like a fight.
You gave, you bleed, you fell so far,
Lost your light, forgot your star.
The mirror's glare, a cruel disguise,
A ghost now stares through tired eyes.
But listen now—just hear me speak,
I know you're tired, I know you're weak.
Yet somewhere deep, beneath the ache,
A fire waits for you to wake.
One last chance—don't turn away,
Not like this, not today.
Rise once more, defy the past,
Give yourself a chance—just one, the last.

To shine, to breathe, to stand so tall,
To prove you never lost it all.

You're not alone. You're stronger than you think. Hold
on. This second chance is yours—Give it a go.

❤

A silent plea

A voice, cracked and aching, calls to the sky,
Begging for answers, pleading, "Why?"
Hands grasp for something that won't stay,
Falling, losing—fading away.
You've fought, you've prayed, you've held on tight,
Yet still, it feels like the world stole your light.
A scream, a whisper, a silent plea—
"Why did You choose this path for me?"
The weight of loss, the endless night,
The fear of endings, the vanished light.
Rage collides with quiet despair,
No answer comes—just empty air.
But then... a pause, a breath, a space,
A quiet warmth, a soft embrace.
Not from above, not from the past,
But deep within—you're home at last.
A voice, small yet strong, appears,
A part of you, untouched by years.
"I know you're hurting, but I am here.
Hold my hand—let's face the fear."

So rest today, just let it be,
Take one step, then two, and three.
The past has passed, the dark will fade,
Look within—the light remains.
You may feel lost, but you're not alone,
Inside, you carry a strength you've always known.
Trust in the light that still burns bright,
Within you, there is always light.

Hey you! Stand up, breathe, and walk toward the light—
one step at a time.
❤

The Third Day's Pain

On the third day, I know the weight feels deep,
A quiet ache that won't let you sleep.
It lingers heavy, thick as air,
A constant reminder of despair.
Your body aches, your heart feels tight,
A soul adrift in endless night.
Questions swirl in a ceaseless flow,
"What could I have done? Why this, I don't know?"
Tears fall soft but don't quite heal,
The wounds inside, they barely feel.
Your mind, a storm of endless thought,
Wrestling with battles that can't be fought.
Each breath a struggle, each step slow,
The path ahead seems unclear, unknown.
How to survive, how to get through?
When every part of you feels askew.
But on the third day, something strange,
Your heart feels broken, yet begins to change.
Not a healing, but a quiet still,
A whisper inside that says, "You have the will."

In the silence, a strength is found,
Not from fighting, but from standing your ground.
The pain still lingers, but it's not the same,
It's now a part of you, not someone to blame.
So on the third day, though it's tough,
Know that surviving is more than enough.
In the ache, in the grief, in the tears that fall,
You are still here, and that is all.

You've made it this far-though the road is hard,
remember you're not alone, and your strength is greater
than you think.

❤

The Healing hands

The ache still feels the same, sharp and deep,
A quiet pain that won't let you sleep.
It wraps around your soul like chains,
A weight that fills both heart and veins.
The world outside moves fast and bright,
But here within, it's an endless night.
Questions swirl in every thought,
"What did I miss? What could I have sought?"
But on this day, something shifts within,
A soft whisper through the winds.
A flicker of light, a breath, a spark,
A gentle voice calling from the dark.
Your heart still heavy, your mind still torn,
But in the quiet, strength is born.
The path ahead may seem unclear,
But courage whispers, "You're still here."
The tears still fall, the sorrow's real,
But in this pain, you start to heal.
Each step is hard, each breath a fight,
But you're beginning to see the light.

The battle rages, the storm won't cease,
But in your heart, there's growing peace.
Though the struggle is far from done,
You find the strength to carry on.
Though doubts may cloud, and fear may rise,
You face them all with open eyes.
You are more than this moment's pain,
And you find yourself whole again.
The road ahead may still be long,
But inside, you're learning to be strong.
With every step, with every breath,
You're finding strength beyond the depth.
So hold your ground, and take each stride,
With courage, let your fears subside.
Though the storm may howl and roar,
You've got the strength to ask for more.
And on this day, the light will glow,
You are stronger than you know.
You may still feel the pain, but you've found,
That in the silence, strength is crowned.

I know it hurts, and everything feels blurry right now.
But hold on, have a little faith—soon, you'll be on the
side of gain.

❤

A Sacred Bond

In the silence where the echoes fade,
A sacred bond is softly laid.
A connection unseen, yet deeply true,
It heals your heart and carries you through.
The hand of grace, so pure, so kind,
Lifts you when life is blind.
A touch that speaks without a sound,
In the stillness, peace is found.
Once lost in darkness, torn and weak,
You think the end is all you'll seek.
But through the storm, you find your way,
A miracle to light the day.
The voices that once roared so loud,
Now soften, like a distant cloud.
Not forgotten, but now at rest,
A quiet light begins its quest.
In your soul, a spark does rise,
A warmth that melts the darkest skies.
Though hope seems faint, you see the glow,
A glimpse of peace begins to show.

God's watching over, taking care,
In moments when you've lost your prayer.
The road ahead is still unclear,
But in your heart, you feel God near.
The winds that once threatened to break,
Now whisper words that you can take.
A steady breath, a gentle sigh,
You feel the strength to still stand high.
And though the night seems long and wide,
You know that light will soon collide.
Every step, each wound and tear,
Has led you here, and the God is near.

Hey God has got your back, and brighter days are just around the corner!

❤

The whisper of the soul

The whisper of your soul, soft and deep,
A voice that stirs memories, secrets to keep.
It speaks of things once left unheard,
Gifts from God and precious words.
As you look back, you see it all,
The times you thought you'd surely fall.
The moments when you felt so small,
Yet in those shadows, God's love stood tall.
There were days when your heart felt torn,
When you thought you'd never been reborn.
But through the pain, through endless night,
God held you close, a constant light.
In every surprise, in every prayer,
God's presence was there, beyond compare.
Through struggles and fears, you lost your way,
But God's gentle hands were there to stay.
You remember the moments so sweet,
When you felt God's love, pure and complete.
Even when doubt clouded your mind,
A higher power was always kind.

You thought you were the unlucky one,
Lost in the dark, with dreams undone.
But now you see, with tearful eyes,
How God's grace was your greatest prize.
Every step, every fall, every climb,
God was with you, all through time.
A silent force, steady and true,
Making your dreams, once distant, come through.
And now, looking back, you know it clear,
That every joy, every tear,
Was God's way of showing, in the deepest pain,
That love will always find a way to sustain.
It's in those memories, both sweet and raw,
That you feel the touch of God's pure law.
Through it all, you've come to see,
God's kindness has always set you free.

Hey, no matter how tough it gets, just remember the best
is yet to come!

❤

Broken But Beautiful

In the quiet of your heart, there's a whisper so deep,
A voice that calls you, even as you weep.
It speaks of strength, hidden in the pain,
Of beauty that rises after the rain.
Your soul, once fractured, now finds its light,
In the darkest of moments, you see the fight.
Though the scars remain, they're not your chains,
They're marks of courage, from enduring the rains.
The pain still lingers, but it doesn't break,
It shapes your spirit, for your own sake.
Every tear that falls, every bruise that stays,
Is a testament to your unspoken praise.
And though you may stumble, and sometimes fall,
You rise again, stronger through it all.
Within you burns a fire so bright,
A promise of hope, a future in sight.
So trust the process, embrace the strain,
In every tear, there's healing from the pain.
Broken, yes, but beautiful too,
Your heart is a masterpiece, born anew.

Hey, you're stronger than you think—keep going, you've
got this!
The world is waiting for you to shine, so don't ever miss.
Each step you take, no matter how small,
Leads you closer to the dreams you'll soon recall.

Hey, you're stronger than you think—keep going, you've
got this!
❤

The Gift of Acceptance

And the day finally comes,
You've accepted what's done.
The past can't be changed,
But you're no longer rearranged.
Two paths lie before you now—
To blame, to linger, or take a bow.
To ask, "Why me?" or let it be,
A chance to move, to set yourself free.
This is no full stop, but a pause,
A comma, not an end, because—
A better future calls your name,
A brighter day, no more the same.
Trust the whispers, trust the light,
Trust the inner spark burning bright.
Take a step, just one for now,
You've hit rock bottom, but you'll rise somehow.
Hold onto hope, though it's thin,
Let each day be where you begin.
No need for leaps, just steady pace,
The future waits, you'll find your place.

A lovely life is waiting for you,
A path that's fresh, a sky so blue.
So take a breath and make your start,
Your journey's just begun, from the heart.
Through every storm, through every tear,
You'll find your strength, and rise from fear.
Though the road ahead may twist and wind,
A beautiful future is yours to find.
So, trust the process, trust the time,
Each step you take is yours to climb.
In your heart, you've always known,
The light will guide you—you're not alone.

Hey, remember no matter how hard it gets, you're never
alone—one step at a time, I believe in you.

♥

The Magic of a New Beginning

There's magic in hitting rock bottom, a strange kind of
grace,
When all seems lost, and you've nowhere to chase.
The world feels heavy, and shadows grow long,
But in that darkness, you find where you belong.
Nothing to see, nothing in sight,
But the end is just a chance to ignite.
It's the moment you realize, you have nothing to lose,
Except the pain that you're ready to choose.
When all seems ended, when hope feels thin,
It's the perfect time to let new life begin.
Push yourself forward, take a breath, take a chance,
A new day's waiting for you to dance.
The path is unclear, but the journey is yours,
One step at a time, through unseen doors.
No more looking back, no more regret,
Just today, just this moment, don't forget.
When you're down to nothing, you've only one choice,
To rise from the ashes and find your true voice.

You have the strength, deep inside your soul,
To rebuild, to renew, to make yourself whole.
So trust in the magic that comes from the fall,
It's there you'll find your heart standing tall.
Take each day as it comes, no need to rush,
You're starting again, and that's more than enough.

One day, one step—you're already on your way, and I
believe in you!

♥

Self-love symphony

It's time for your self-love symphony,
A celebration of who you're meant to be.
Your inner child, waiting for your care,
Has been crying in corners, feeling unaware.
So go to them now, embrace so tight,
Whisper, "I see you," in the quiet night.
Tell them you love them, feel the peace,
Hold them close, let the pain cease.
A gentle kiss upon their brow,
"I'll make you proud, I promise now."
Pat their back, let them feel seen,
You are the love they've always dreamed.
"I'm going to make all your dreams come true,
You'll see me living the life you always knew.
Every wish, every hope, you thought would fade,
I'll stand beside you, together we'll invade."
With every step, we'll rise so high,
And you'll watch me reach for the sky.
In every victory, you'll feel the glow,
We'll Walk together, letting the love flow.

No more hiding, no more fear,
You're here now, and you're always near.
Take the lead, it's time to show,
The love that's yours, let it overflow.
From now on, it's you and them,
Together, stronger than you've ever been.
A bond renewed, a heart restored,
Your inner child, now adored.
So together we'll grow, together we'll soar,
Through every challenge, we'll ask for more.
With each dream fulfilled, you'll smile with pride,
For I'll always have you by my side.

Hey, I'm here for you, always, and together we're going
to make all your dreams come true.
❤

Magical moments

You start to see the miracles, small and bright,
In every little thing, in the softest light.
The sun's warm glow, the rain's soft kiss,
These everyday blessings you no longer miss.
The world seems brighter, the air more clear,
Though pain still lingers, hope is near.
In the simplest moments, you find your peace,
Your heart, though wounded, finds release.
A story shared, a life laid bare,
And suddenly, your burden seems lighter to bear.
You realize your pain, though real and deep,
Is less than what you thought, and you start to leap.
Through every struggle, through every tear,
You're learning to see what's always been here.
A different perspective, a heart full of grace,
You're finding beauty in every space.
The days seem softer, the nights less long,
You feel the rhythm, the pulse of your song.
Though life is hard, you know you'll rise,
With every challenge, you'll reach new skies.

So, walk with courage, and let it flow,
Every day, you're learning to grow.
With each step, you're finding light,
In the darkest moments, you shine so bright.
The journey may be long, but you're not alone,
With every step, you're closer to home.
In the quiet, in the struggle, you'll always find,
That strength and love are yours to bind.

And remember, you're doing amazing step by step,
you're creating a life full of light and love, and I'm so
proud of you.

❤

Meeting Myself

In the stillness, I finally sit,
Gathering courage, bit by bit.
To spend time with the one I've known,
But never truly called my own.
I know the world's favorites, the joys they seek,
But what about me? What makes me unique?
What do I crave, what makes me whole?
For the first time, I meet my soul.
It feels strange, unfamiliar too,
Like meeting a stranger, yet it's me, it's true.
A flutter of nerves, a gentle sigh,
A moment to pause, to ask why.
What makes me laugh, what makes me feel,
What dreams are mine that I can heal?
This journey's new, but so profound,
As I listen to my heart's soft sound.
I sit with myself, embracing the space,
Finding comfort in my own grace.
Each breath a step toward inner peace,
A quiet moment, a sweet release.

The discomfort fades, the calm is near,
I start to see things clearly, my dear.
I've spent so long lost in the race,
But now, I find strength in my own embrace.
This is the moment, the one I've missed,
The chance to connect, to feel truly kissed
By my own love, my own gentle hand,
Learning to be, learning to stand.
I'm proud of this silence, proud of this day,
For meeting myself, I've found my way.
A journey begun, no longer alone,
Form now, I am truly, fully my own.

Hey, taking the time to know yourself is such a beautiful
step, and it's so wonderful to see you embracing it!
♥

Falling In Love with Yourself

Each day you spend with yourself, you'll see,
A different side of who you're meant to be.
No longer seeking others' praise,
You'll be amazed at how bright you've become in your
own gaze.
Oh my God, how amazing you are,
A heart so pure, a soul that shines like a star.
A person full of love, who just wants to share,
Spreading happiness, with kindness everywhere.
You radiate joy, and love is your guide,
Filling the world with warmth, no need to hide.
You've never met someone quite like you,
And now, you see the beauty inside, so wild and true.
Why didn't you notice this version before?
How could you have missed it, when you're so much
more?
This friendship with yourself is such a delight,
With each passing day, you're shining bright.
You now know what makes you smile,

You've been with yourself all this while.
You've learned what lingers in your mind,
And found the peace you thought you'd never find.
It's incredible, this feeling you embrace,
Falling in love with yourself at your own pace.
You see all the dreams you've always held near,
A special phase, a new chapter clear.
You look back at the little you,
And see everything you were meant to do.
Childhood dreams now feel so real,
You finally know what it means to heal.
You're becoming your best friend, it's true,
This journey's the best, and it's just you and you.
Every day is a gift, a chance to grow,
Falling in love with yourself—what a beautiful glow.

Hey, you're doing great, and I just know this self-love
journey is gonna bring you all sorts of amazing things!
❤

The Art of Letting Go

You've come so far, and I see you rise,
With a courageous heart and shining eyes.
The fear that once held you, kept you tight,
Now fades away as love fills your light.
You're learning the art of letting go,
Releasing the past, letting it flow.
You're realizing now, holding on too tight,
Only keeps you from embracing the light.
With every step, you shed the weight,
Of all the things that sealed your fate.
You're lighter, freer, full of grace,
Embracing the present, finding your space.
The past no longer holds you down,
You've planted new roots, you've found your crown.
The future is bright, but now you see,
The magic is in the now, in just *being free.*
You've faced your fears, and let them go,
You stand tall, your heart begins to glow.
With love in your soul and peace in your mind,
You've found a strength, so beautifully kind.

So here you are, strong and bold,
Learning that letting go is pure gold.
You've given yourself the freedom to grow,
And now, the world's yours to let your love flow.
You trust yourself more than before,
Opening your heart, feeling the roar
Of life and love, so wild and free,
And you know, deep down, you're exactly where you're
meant to be.
You're living with courage, with love as your guide,
Finding joy and peace with nothing to hide.
The future may call, but now you know,
The true magic lives in today's glow.

Hey, I just know awesome things are headed your way
with every step you take!
❤

Manifesting Your Dreams

Your mind is focused, clear, and bright,
Dreams shining ahead, within your sight.
No longer do you carry the weight,
Your growth and goals are your new fate.
The past no longer holds you down,
You're chasing dreams, no time to frown.
The pain still lingers, but it's far away,
You've found a path, a brighter day.
Your heart is set on making it right,
Focusing on what fills you with light.
You think of your inner child, so pure,
Determined to make them feel secure.
All that matters now is your rise,
Chasing dreams, reaching for the skies.
The world around may still hold its strain,
But in your heart, you feel no pain.
Your only concern is growth, not fear,
You push ahead, the future's clear.
The struggles of the past, now distant,
They've lost their hold, no longer persistent.

Every day you work, you move with grace,
Building the life you're meant to embrace.
Your dreams are real, they're within your reach,
You're learning more with each step you teach.
Your heart beats stronger, fueled by desire,
You're chasing your dreams, you're building fire.
The pain is there, but it no longer binds,
It's fading away, as peace fills your mind.
Now you're focused, you know your way,
The future's bright, you're here to stay.
You're manifesting, and every step you take,
Brings you closer to the life you'll make.

Hello, keep going, you're on the right path—your dreams
are closer than you think, and you've got this!

❤

Dancing With Change

At first, change felt like a heavy weight,
You wondered how you'd navigate.
But now, with every step you take,
You find the rhythm, you learn to break.
Each day you wake, ready to face,
The challenges life brings with grace.
No five-year plan, just the next step clear,
You move forward, knowing there's no fear.
You're working on your dreams, small but true,
Balancing work, pain, and all you pursue.
The hours once felt like a never-ending race,
Now you're managing, you've found your space.
The days stretch long, but they feel so wide,
You're learning to manage, with yourself by your side.
Every little effort, every small thing,
Build the life you're dreaming, it's your own wings.
At first, you doubted, unsure how to cope,
Now you see your dreams and feel more hope.
Your inner child smiles with pride and cheer,
As you take those steps, you're conquering the fear.

You don't need to know it all right now,
You're trusting the process, taking it slow.
Each day is a chance, each hour a gift,
You're learning to let your heart lift.
You're motivating yourself, with every stride,
Your inner strength no longer has to hide.
You've got the courage to keep going through,
No matter the challenge, you'll see it through.
And as you dance with change, you realize,
You're growing stronger with each sunrise.
Life is unfolding, you're finding your way,
And every step you take leads to a brighter day.

Hey, keep dancing with change and trust that every step
is bringing you closer to the life you're meant to live!
❤

Finally Free

Once, change felt like a daunting dance,
A rhythm I couldn't quite embrace,
The steps were awkward, the moves unsure,
But now, I'm dancing with grace.
What once felt heavy, now feels light,
I move with joy, no longer shy,
My inner child is smiling wide,
As we twirl beneath the sky.
The beat of change now fills my soul,
It lifts me high, it makes me whole,
The fear I had is fading fast,
I'm finally free, and free at last.
I've learned to dance through every storm,
To find the beauty in each form,
Embracing what once brought me fear,
Now fills my heart with love so clear.
I'm responsible for all my joy,
For the happiness I now employ,
I spread it wide with every move,
In every step, my heart does prove.

For the first time, I see my face,
And in the mirror, there's no trace,
Of doubt or worry, just pure pride,
I've grown and blossomed from inside.
Tears fall, but they're not from pain,
They're tears of joy, a sweet refrain,
I've made myself proud today,
Dancing freely, come what may.
So here I stand, no longer small,
Embracing change, I stand so tall,
For in this dance, I've found my way,
And with each step, I greet the day.

Hey, dancing with change, you've found your rhythm,
and look at you—glowing from within!
♥

Second Chance-A spiritual power

With unshakable faith, you trusted the divine,
And now you see how things align.
Your prayers were heard, your heart was seen,
From "Why me?" to "Thank you" — you've been redeemed.
God showed you the strength deep inside,
Instead of stumbling, you chose to rise.
You gave yourself a second chance,
And now you lead with a fearless stance.
The path wasn't easy, but you found your way,
Each challenge faced, each choice to stay.
Now you stand tall, a story to tell,
Of how you rose, how you broke the spell.
You've become the main character of your own tale,
No longer bound by fear, you set sail.
The light you sought is now shining bright,
As you embrace your truth, your inner light.
Look at what you've come through, what you've become,
A warrior, a dreamer, no longer numb.

Every step, every lesson, you took with grace,
And now you stand in your rightful place.
Your journey has shaped you, strong and free,
A version of yourself you were destined to be.
With every scar, every tear that fell,
You grew into the hero of your own spell.
So now, see the power you hold within,
The best version of you, let the story begin.
With faith and strength, you've come so far,
You've become the brightest, most radiant star.

Hey, keep dancing with change and trust that every step
is bringing you closer to the life you're meant to live!

❤

The Power of Choice

Choice is a power, a gift so divine,
A privilege granted, a spark that will shine.
It shapes your life, it carves your way,
Every decision is a step toward a new day.
Don't fear the wrong, the path untried,
For each choice, you learn to glide.
The journey's not perfect, it's part of the flow,
In every misstep, you begin to grow.
Choice is the centerpiece of your fate,
It molds your world, it opens the gate.
You have the power to create your life,
To turn the chaos into peace, the struggle into light.
I know it's hard, the road seems steep,
But remember, you've climbed mountains so deep.
You've fought battles tougher than this,
And emerged stronger, with grace and bliss.
The strength inside, it never fades,
It grows with each challenge, with every wave.
You've faced the storm, and you've walked the night,
And now, you rise with your inner light.

You have a choice in every single day,
To turn the dark into brighter rays.
The power is yours, it's never lost,
Your choices shape you, no matter the cost.
So stand tall, with courage in your soul,
You have the strength to make yourself whole.
Every choice is a step, and you're not alone,
With each decision, you're closer to your throne.
Keep moving forward, trust your inner guide,
In every choice, let love be your stride.
You've fought harder battles, you've come so far,
With the power of choice, you'll reach your star.

You're doing awesome—every choice you make is one
step closer to the life you're meant to live, and I'm
cheering you on!

❤

The Hurdles You've Crossed

Life's felt like a race, hasn't it?
A trail of hurdles, tall and steep,
Each one harder, each one a test,
Making you wonder if you'd ever leap.
At first, they seemed like giants, too high,
Stronger than you, you'd doubt and fall,
But with each jump, you gained new might,
Each stumble taught you to stand tall.
The sweat, the tears, it all felt too much,
But you kept moving, step by step,
Though at times the finish seemed so far,
You pushed on, no time to rest.
With every breath, you found the way,
A rhythm, a pace, a strength untold,
Now the hurdles still stand before,
But they no longer feel so bold.
You've learned to leap with grace and trust,
To move with faith, through doubt's dark veil,
The finish line's in sight, at last,
And you've earned every step without fail.

Tears fall, but not from defeat,
These are tears of victory's glow,
You've crossed the toughest, hardest parts,
And now, at the line, you know.
This race was never just the end,
It's all the moments that shaped you strong,
The pain, the growth, each lesson learned,
Now you see it was all along.
You did this for you, and for them too,
For the child who once feared the race,
Now cheering loud, so proud, so true,
Seeing strength in every trace.
This win is yours, a battle fought,
A victory from deep inside,
With faith, with kindness, strength anew,
You stand proud, with nothing to hide.

Hey buddy, Look at you go! You've come so far, and this
is just the beginning—keep shining!
❤

God's Favourite Child: The Chosen One

You've faced your fears, each one a shadow,
That whispered doubts, but you let them go.
In every moment, you found your grace,
A quiet faith, a steady pace.
Through storms and trials, you stood tall,
You knew deep within, you'd never fall.
The magic of now, the power of today,
Unfolded in the smallest ways.
Each breath, each step, a gift divine,
The alchemy of love, transforming time.
Turning pain to wisdom, turning hurt to light,
You rose from the ashes, stronger, bright.
You met your fears with open arms,
They couldn't shake you, couldn't cause harm.
You knew inside, you were enough,
And you were made of something tough.
You were becoming the best you could be,
And every scar sets your spirit free.
Your inner child danced with joy,

Proud of the journey, proud of the fight.
No longer afraid, no longer lost,
You embraced your strength, no matter the cost.
For every tear shed, for every night alone,
Was a step toward finding your true home.
God was with you, guiding your way,
Protecting your heart, lighting your day.
In every challenge, you saw the plan,
A perfect design, made by God's hand.
You were the warrior, chosen with care,
To carry the weight, to stand and declare.
And now you see the reason why,
You faced the storm, you reached the sky.
God found you the toughest of all,
And through your battles, you stand tall.
You fought not alone, but with divine might,
A warrior of love, a beacon of light.
In the quiet, you understood your worth,
You were born to rise, born to birth
A strength no one could ever steal,
A power, unshaken, forever real.
Now you stand, a vision of grace,
You have found your sacred place.
The trials were not meant to break,
But to awaken, for your own sake.
Through suffering, you found your soul,
Now you walk towards your goal.

You are more than you ever knew,
A creation divine, in all you do.
God's plan was bigger than you could see,
He chose you for this, He chose you to be free.
Through every storm, you gained your wings,
Now you soar on wings of powerful things.
With love in your heart, and faith in your soul,
You're stepping into the highest role.
The magic is real, the blessings surround,
You're living the life you were meant to be found.
Every moment a gift, every breath a sign,
You are God's favourite, and the journey is yours.
The path ahead is clear, the future so bright,
You are the chosen, born for this fight.
You are God's favoured child, the chosen one,
The battle was tough, but now it's done.
You stand here proud, not just to survive,
But to thrive, to soar, to truly arrive.
With faith, with love, with strength so grand,
You Walk into your destiny, guided by His hand.
You are God's favourite child, the chosen one,
Destined for greatness, your journey has just begun.

Hey, take on the future with all the strength and
confidence you've got! The best is yet to come! Blessings
and Blessings..